When Sexual Harassment Feels Like Prostitution

Volume II

SEXUAL HARASSMENT IS...

By J. Anita Lafayette

Sexual Harassment Is...

Disclaimer and Terms of Use: Each person decides individually when obtaining a lawyer is needed. This book does not replace legal counsel a lawyer provides.

Library of Congress (Submitted In 2010)

ISBN 1451543700 and EAN-13 9781451543704

Printed in the United States of America by KDP an Amazon.com company.

Jacqueline_Lafayette@yahoo.com

WHEN SEXUAL HARASSMENT FEELS LIKE PROSTITUTION:

Volume II

Sexual Harassment Is...

Table of Contents

Introduction

SEXUAL HARASSMENT IS A MAJOR PROBLEM

The purpose of this book is to make sexual harassment a much easier topic of discussion. SEXUAL HARASSMENT IS written for the millions of working adults and teenagers. SEXUAL HARASSMENT IS in print to be a tool to hold open sexual harassment training sessions. Sexual harassment does not have to be the dreadful legal topic of discussion all the time. SEXUAL HARASSMENT IS a book to help build stronger and more positive working environments. SEXUAL HARASSMENT IS a small manuscript about company management being transparent in acknowledging this huge coast to coast problem and company management's willingness to deal with sexual harassment more straightforwardly. Why annually lose $150,000 to millions in lawsuit damages and only improve monitoring of computers, e-mails, and phone calls better?

Transparency is not always easy, but may create less hostile work environments in the future for all employees. Your employees will respect company management for straightforwardly speaking about these issues. Transparency within company management might be the beginning of changing the statistics of peer to peer sexual harassment. When leadership is seen out front similar to a lighthouse on the water's shoreline openly communicating issues, leaders make tremendous changes within businesses. My goal is to change SEXUAL HARASSMENT IS to sexual harassment was a major problem. I believe every employee should have a copy of this book.

Statistical data shows 1 out of 2 sexual harassment cases reported are company managers or supervisors (1). SEXUAL HARASSMENT IS a major problem in the workplace. Dealing with sexual harassment for over a decade had allowed this victim to see the selfish act of sexual harassment too many times. SEXUAL HARASSMENT IS a form of discrimination. SEXUAL HARASSMENT IS illegal and SEXUAL HARASSMENT IS a lot more. This tool defines sexual harassment in broader terms.

The sexual harassers cost companies we work for hundreds of thousands to millions of dollars in lawsuits. The sexual harassers destroy the lives of their victims. This list addresses how the sexual harassers are allowed to operate, because he or she is just expressing an exaggerated social personality.

Sexual harassment feels like prostitution and a lot more from a victim's perspective. In my first book, When Sexual Harassment Feels Like Prostitution volume one, I had dealt with the attacks the supervisors and managers had launched at this subordinate employee. I had to clearly communicate the hideousness of the sexual dominance confrontations by company management. I had to get the sexual harassment monkey off my back because that horrible stuff kept coming back. A decade is long enough to have to endure sexual harassment repeatedly, plus I was made to feel like I did not have a voice or a right to better treatment. When Sexual Harassment Feels Like

Prostitution; in my first book I had written I expected better treatment and my payroll is strictly for my job description.

Many employees, who are sexually harassed by a manager or a supervisor, are an emotional wreck long before he or she seeks help. The feeling of prostituting for money is a horrible position to be placed in, but the information regarding hostile-environment harassment, quid pro quo harassment, a favor-for-a-favor harassment, and finally this-for-that harassment situations are not communicated in these words, on-the-job prostitution. It is time for a more assertive dialog to match this dilemma. If company management is statistically 50% of the problem, this topic needs broader ways to convey. What are these manager's personal expectations from his or her subordinate employees, if company management is 1 out of 2 of the cases reported? This is a good question.

SEXUAL HARASSMENT IS written to help rebuild the victim's lost self-esteem. This book is about never losing your confidence, even if you find yourself in a hostile environment. Employees and company management need to understand the tremendous burden and war waged at the sexually harassed employee's feet. If you are an employee with health issues, the sexual harassment attacks can be more harmful and emotionally damaging. I was an employee who had dealt with sexual harassment and health issues, too. How fair is that? What if a female is in the early stages of pregnancy? Hostile environments are not fair. The term; sexual harassment, is a candy label for many people and this book explains candy label a little more towards the end of this book.

The statistic of sexual harassment encounters from a manager or a supervisor in my case is around 75%. Everyone pays a price for the sexual harassment behavior in the workplace. Who is carrying the burden of this behavior in most cases? I have been a victim without a voice, plus thousands more victims go unheard annually. Who is paying the huge monetary price for this crime in most cases? If you are a victim of sexual harassment and lost a job; you have paid a price. Companies are paying a huge price in lawsuits.

The person on the defensive side has a right to say I am not interested and no thank you. All sexually aggressiveness should end without repercussions. The employee and manager should be able to return to work without further conflicts, but some sexually hostile people cannot move forward, act professional, and let go. If companies take a firmer stance against sexual harassment and organize easier trouble-free arbitration meetings for the employees, this might improve the sexual harassment statistics, plus this might save the company money.

Why are some sexually harassed victims still losing his or her employment? What if the human resources (HR) department offered in writing no whistleblower damages by the company will occur, a strong leadership example to the victim for reporting sexual harassment, who has clearly communicated the problem coming from a supervisor or a manager? This is goodwill during an investigation. If a diligent employee or dependable employee returns to work for the same manager, some intervention and oversight is needed for the employee's protection. Intervention like the manager has to have the Human Resources Manager or Director in all future meetings dealing with the victim's performance.

If a lawsuit is not filed, the employee feels valued, and the employee's job has been protected on paper then all parties win. The employee can go home and sleep a little better. The protected employee would still have to meet the expectations of job performance like quality work and being on time, if he or she decides to remain with the company.

SEXUAL HARASSMENT IS written to peel off the layers of complexity regarding this problem, explain sexual harassment simply, and uncover the war waged at the subordinate employees' feet. SEXUAL HARASSMENT IS written to explain the attacks clearly so everyone can see the devastating attack any adult or any teenager faces when he or she is confronted with a sexually aggressive boss at work. By the time you get to the end of this book, you will be able to say "SEXUAL HARASSMENT IS..." and you will understand this topic a bit better.

Chapter 1

SEXUAL HARASSMENT IS...

Sexual Harassment Is Prostitution Sometimes

I like sticking to the exact definitions for the words listed below. I prefer the sexual harassment problem to be explained in more than one way. I have described sexual harassment as more than just being illegal or discrimination. SEXUAL HARASSMENT IS a war wage and the weapons are an arsenal of psychological abuse the victim has to endure. The war waged causes illness and sleepless nights. By defining the problem of sexual harassment in broader terms, the weapons used against the victims are better seen. SEXUAL HARASSMENT IS also prostitution in some situations. If a manager or a supervisor suggests in any form your payroll received is a payment for sexual favors too, this is the hostile-environment harassment, this is also discrimination, and can lead to quid pro quo harassment, if the manager now basis his or her decisions from the unsatisfactory or satisfactory results of sexual advances; well that is prostitution in a few carefully extracted definitions from Merriam Webster's dictionary. My two books are communicating sexual harassment from the victim's experience, from the victim's eyes and ears. I am explaining this in simple terms. What makes some forms of sexual harassment prostitution?

Solicit (a)

"1 a : to make petition to: entreat

b : to approach with a request or plea

2 : to urge (as one's cause) strongly 3 a : to entice or lure
  especially into evil

b : to proposition (someone) especially as or in the
character

of a prostitute 4 : to try to obtain by usually urgent requests
or pleas" (a)

Prostitute (b)

"1 : to offer indiscriminately for sexual intercourse
Especially for money.

2 : to devote to corrupt or unworthy purposes : debase" (b)

Debase (c)

"1 : to lower in status, esteem, quality, or character

Sexual Harassment (d)

"1 : uninvited and unwelcome verbal or physical behavior

of a sexual nature especially by a person in authority

toward a subordinate (as an employee or student)" (d).

Sexual Harassment Is About Control

If you are forced to do anything, you are being controlled. When you are standing or sitting near a co-worker, whose unwelcomed sexual harassing manner repeats, a large room becomes very small really quick. If you are backed into a corner by the sexual harasser, the closed in confrontational area or space is to control you, the victim. The confrontation in your face is all about control.

You need to see a hostile confrontation as an attempt to control you, the victim. Your emotions are being challenged negatively. The hostile confrontation is to put you on the defense, to intimidate, to cause you to fear the hostile individual, and the aggressive sexual harasser wants you, the victim to give into them. How many times were you made to endure being touched? How many times did you endure being spoken to inappropriately?

If you are standing or sitting, another person starts touching you, and this is unwelcomed; you are being told by the physical contact; you, the victim has to endure the physical touching. If you feel like a contact sport or a playground for touching due to the exercised routines of the aggressor, you are being controlled. The sexual harasser touches you and you are supposed to like it, you are supposed to think the touching is cute, and you are not supposed to move, then you are being controlled.

That situation rehearsed over and over communicates the sexual harasser is in control over that particular situation.

Excuse me, please do not touch me is in order. Request the other person to exercise a polite and respectful distance. You are in control when you request a respectful distance. You are in control when you request the other person is to act professional. If control is going to be exercised, I say use your control and request respect at all times. You cannot change the other person, but you can control who touches you.

I have dealt with a lot of the psychological controlling garbage to keep an income. I did not put up with that touchy controlling stuff. My patience for being touched is on a real short fuse. The dominating control in the form of touching has the hairs on my back standing up very quickly. The touching control move expressed by sexual harasser goes too far. I do not like feeling like a contact sport playground. I prefer respectful means of communication.

Sexual Harassment Is About Money Control

Sexual harassment destroys business and professional relationships. The numerous times I had been sexually harassed by a boss had put me in an awkward position. The touching was not a work performance review and that was not a general how your day is going greeting. The boss has the money and the boss has a personal proposition for you, let's get personal and close.

The chances are the boss has already had sexual harassment training. Sexual harassment training is required in new hire orientations, companies hold sexual harassment training annually, or specialized sexual harassment seminars for the company management. Many company managers have a very good understanding of sexual harassment from working and training.

Why would the boss sexually harass anyone? If the boss is well trained, why is the boss sexually confrontational with any subordinate? Are the advances to control the person in general or exercise a monetary control? Why are managers sexually harassing his or her employees? These are very good questions. The boss is deliberately destroying the business and the professional relationship with his or her employee. That action has a direct impact on the employee's chances for a promotion, continuing employment, and future raises. Company superiors make up 50% of the sexual harassment cases and superiors do not know he or she is negatively hurting the subordinate employee's future. I think this is known.

Sexual Harassment Is Abusive Behavior

Hostile behavior is abusive behavior. If you have to put up with sexual harassment, the aggressor is being extremely rude. The sexual harasser is ignoring all professional codes of conduct at work. When you have been approached more than one time by the same sexual harasser, the harasser only cares about his or her level of enjoyment, which is being sexually confrontational with you and ignores the victim's feeling altogether.

Sexual Harassment Is Aggressive Behavior

SEXUAL HARASSMENT IS unwanted attention. The aggressive behavior does not deserve to be smiled at. Aggressive people are looking for the opportunity to control a situation. Aggressive behavior demands to control the situation and you, the victim is supposed to just smile and allow intimate things to happen.

Sexual Harassment Is Appalling

Do employees only see his or her hand in the "cookie jar" or may be the "candy jar" of sex play at work? You, the victim should recognize unprofessional behavior and do not absorb guilt over another individual's actions. The behavior of a sexual harasser does not redefine your value. To deal with sexual harassment repeatedly is appalling.

Sexual Harassment Is Attacking Behavior

Your personal barriers are being torn down when you are being sexually harassed. Sexual harassment can be overly

aggressive behavior when that behavior has not been put in check or stopped. Everyone, who has ever played any physical contact sport, knows the offense position, the aggressive forward actions, or the movements are out in front to attack. The sexual harasser is way out in front of the action and the action is not welcomed. You, the victim is caught off guard, blind-sided, or placed into uncomfortable situations.

Sexual Harassment Is Awful

The offensive action of SEXUAL HARASSMENT IS not acceptable. Just the opposite occurs when you are sexually harassed; feelings of extreme disagreement or objection to the hostile activity are felt. The fear of losing your job because you are a sexually harassed victim is awful.

Sexual Harassment Is Bondage

Sexual harassment that is vile in action communicates a mind that is filled with sexual bondage. The sexual harasser cannot escape the reoccurring thoughts, which has him or her repeating that behavior and those actions destroy business relationships. Some people are bound to drugs or alcohol. At work, the repeating sexually aggressive person is bound to the despicable acts he or she outwardly displays, which demands another person's unwilling attention.

Sexual Harassment Is Bullying

The sexual harasser knows about bullying others or being bullied from years of dealing with peers at school, in sports events, from educational resources, and in training courses. Dominating behavior launched at the victim to intimidate and cause fear is bullying. Cats, dogs, and children even do this with each other. Adults come to work and express bullying behavior, which is horrible to bring into the workplace. Bullying at work makes the work environment a negative office culture.

Sexual Harassment Is Corruption

Corruption in this instance is the moral compass of the sexual harasser that is lost. Corruption is destroyed integrity, missing virtue, and the ruined moral principles for the harasser. The numbers of people whose lives are impacted by sexual harassment see the corruption in the workplace up close. I have seen this corruption inside many businesses. One bad apple can spoil a bunch, or a place to work really quickly. If the sexual harasser is in your face constantly, the one bad apple makes working at that particular company difficult.

Sexual Harassment Is Degrading

Your professional value as an employee is being lowered. Sexual harassment directly peels away your self-esteem and professional ranking in the workplace. Your significance has been lowered to a sex playmate. Anyone enduring one or more encounters of SEXUAL HARASSMENT IS degraded by the rude confrontations.

Sexual Harassment Is Demeaning

The sexually harassed victim's character has been devalued. The professional employment status of the harassed is also being placed under attack and deliberately changed by the sexual harassment actions. When you can identify how much you have been insulted and have not allowed the sexual harasser's behavior to give you ulcers; you have done well. Fighting back can be powerful. Fighting back does not have to be hostile or

threatening. Empowering yourself with information to fight back on a psychological level can mean resting a bit better.

Sexual Harassment Is Deplorable

Many in the workplace are not happy about the vile, the bullying, and the disrespectful behavior in the workplace. One bad apple would definitely be classified as deplorable. One selfish sexually vile person can ruin things for the victim and a really nice workplace.

Sexual Harassment Is Discrimination

You can keep your job, if you have sex with the boss. That action communicates a prejudice in employees. The boss is responding differently to you in a sexual way. Your qualifications have dropped to a measurement standard of sexual or intimate activities for a paycheck, due to hostile-environment harassment, a favor-for-a-favor harassment, this-for-that harassment, or prostitution in the workplace. If your job performance, duties, and responsibilities are also based on passionate or intimate time with the boss, this is discrimination.

Sexual Harassment Is Dreadful

SEXUAL HARASSMENT IS not pleasant. The victim begins to hate going to work and having to deal with the sexually focused individual that shows up without fail. The victim is dreading another sexual encounter with a peer or with the boss. A little sex play at work is a "candy jar" and the sexual harasser is a "happy camper", until some kind of disciplinary action is taken, but many stakeholders suffer too. The victim dreads the sexual harassment and the risk of getting fired for being a victim in the situation, which causes a lot of emotional suffering for the victim on a daily basis.

Sexual Harassment Is Hateful

The individual doing the sexual harassment many times are being mean in a sleazy manner. The sexual harasser may have some negative issues. This could be a form of resentment over the employee's professional appearance and polite or polished mannerism in the workplace. SEXUAL HARASSMENT IS a weapon and a tongue hanging sign for being sexually aroused.

Sexual Harassment Is Hounding Behavior

The hounding behavior can show up in a stalking kind of action. I said earlier that I needed to get the monkey off of my back. No human being likes the feeling of being hounded. There is not anything pleasant about sexual harassment. This book's list clearly points this out.

Sexual Harassment Is Humiliating

Please stop humiliating me. How many people say that at work? It is very humiliating to be sexually harassed. Now an employee, who is dependable and a hard-working employee is feeling really close to being terminated for being sexually harassed. The anxiety mounts for the victim being harassed. Help and goodwill actions are needed to restore the confidence of the employee, who is also a valued member of the company.

Sexual Harassment Is Illegal

SEXUAL HARASSMENT IS unauthorized conduct displayed that is unlawful to exhibit at work or in positions of authority.

Sexual Harassment Is Impolite Behavior

SEXUAL HARASSMENT IS impolite and displays a lack of restraint. Sexual harassment has a cut and dry way of looking at it. SEXUAL HARASSMENT IS discrimination, illegal, and it can disrupt the victim's life greatly. The sexual harasser is ill-mannered and rude. This list is designed to empower your psychological framework and separate the poor treatment from your self-worth.

Sexual Harassment Is Insulting

When I had to look at repeated vile gestures it was insulting. If you are being touched and you do not want to be touched, that is insulting. The sexual harasser's human value totally exceeds the victim's human value or employment value is very insulting. SEXUAL HARASSMENT IS cruel.

Sexual Harassment Is Offensive Behavior

SEXUAL HARASSMENT IS an act of poor judgment. Our culture in general and the business culture, both teach to cease from offensive behavior. The professional relationship you and your manager are supposed to have has now changed. Total disrespect for the subordinate is displayed, when the sexual harassment continues.

Sexual Harassment Is Oppressive Behavior

The behavior is not fair. The behavior is domineering. SEXUAL HARASSMENT IS designed to hold the victim down and to set up traps for the victim to excel less in life. To deliberately hold another individual back is an act of oppression.

Sexual Harassment Is Rude Behavior

Obnoxious and rude also describes the behavior of a sexual harasser. To be rude is to show no respect. The sexual harasser is communicating by his or her behavior; he or she is not going to respect you, the victim.

Sexual Harassment Is Serious

If the sexually harassed victim is losing sleep and fears losing his or her job, SEXUAL HARASSMENT IS serious. If company managers or supervisors are 50% of the problem, plus he or she feels an entitlement to sexual favors because they have an employee receiving a monetary benefit from a paycheck, this is serious. Companies cannot stop managers or supervisors from

thinking that way because the "moral compass" of some people are unfortunately corrupted or lost. Companies can train everyone on prostitution in the workplace. Prostitution or sexual harassment in the workplace is a serious topic and needs to be addressed straightforwardly.

Sexual Harassment Is Shameful

Some people at work are ashamed he or she knows a peer, who is a sexual harasser. If your company has an anonymous employee tip-line to report problems in the workplace, pick up the phone, call to report sexual harassment, and the bullying in the workplace. Much of these feelings can be changed by taking action and reporting all acts of sexual harassment, so that victims can have his or her life back. Sometimes sexual harassment situations need a voice to speak up and help defend the countless victims.

Sexual Harassment Is Terrible

Statistical data shows 1 out of 2 sexual harassment cases reported is company management (1). What can be worse? Statistical data reflecting not 50%, but becomes 60%-70% of the

reported cases are company managers or supervisors. SEXUAL HARASSMENT IS a major problem. In my books, When Sexual Harassment Feels Like Prostitution; volumes one and two will hopefully lower the statistic of sexual harassment originating from company management, who are 50% of the reported cases. SEXUAL HARASSMENT IS a terrible situation, either from a superior or a peer. These attacks from superiors have a more devastating impact on employees.

Sexual Harassment Is Unacceptable

Sexual harassment should not be tolerated. Expressing the term sexual harassment in everyday terms is to identify the problem on a broader scale, to detail the various emotions, to help others see a different view, and hopefully have more people speaking up in the future. SEXUAL HARASSMENT IS an unacceptable behavior.

Sexual Harassment Is Unbecoming

In some circles, tongue hanging remarks are a part of the group's language. Both, men and women have their own language for aroused senses. Instead of unbecoming, the sexual

harasser's language and behavior express a language that is acceptable. SEXUAL HARASSMENT IS not flattering to all recipients.

Sexual Harassment Is Not Pleasant

If we could deal with all the unpleasant things in life, make the problems disappear, and have no stress days; life would be nice. My goal is to open new dialog for sexual harassment and remove some of the unpleasantness. My goal is to suggest goodwill frameworks to be set up and offered to the sexually harassed employees. Can arbitration be easier meetings of diplomacy? The HR department and company management should address poor job performance, but protect the careers of the sexually harassed victims with aggressive goodwill frameworks to restore the employees' feeling of being valued in the workplace. My goal is to help the sexually harassed employees build long lasting careers, which now are cut short for reporting the occurrences of sexual harassment attacks. Some victims still lose his or her employment shortly after reporting sexual harassment and this is wrong.

Sexual Harassment Is Wrong

The sexual harassment attacks create a hostile work environment. The bullying and the various acts taken to control the victim are wrong. In this book, SEXUAL HARASSMENT IS, I am comparing discrimination and prostitution, plus detailing other issues. SEXUAL HARASSMENT IS affecting company cultures negatively. SEXUAL HARASSMENT IS a multifaceted problem. Why are the victims losing employment?

Sexual harassment has been the ugly legal topic for discussion. What if sexual harassment training was designed around building a more positive workplace cultures? What if sexual harassment training was done to allow employees to really discuss the topic openly? What if all employees chipped in to guard the workplace from bullying and sexual harassment? What if, more offensive steps were designed to make the workplace a safer and less hostile environment? Who says we cannot improve the sexual harassment statistics? My goal is to change SEXUAL

HARASSMENT IS a major problem to sexual harassment was a major problem.

Sexual Harassment Is About Goodwill

SEXUAL HARASSMENT IS a manuscript about restoring the value of employees, whose team worth and team value has been lost due to sexual harassment encounters. SEXUAL HARASSMENT IS a short book about finding goodwill ambassadors within companies and company management being transparent in dealing with this problem of sexual harassment coming from the rankings of managers and supervisors. SEXUAL HARASSMENT IS a compelling book about designing goodwill frameworks for employees to come directly to HR quickly; before the employee's health deteriorates and loses sleep from the abuses of sexual harassment. SEXUAL HARASSMENT IS a ground-breaking book about the Human Resources department tackling this very expensive and unpleasant situation with an easy to understand resource. SEXUAL HARASSMENT IS a book about taking the candy label off of the term, sexual harassment. In this book, SEXUAL HARASSMENT IS, the person-to-person illegal dealing candy store operating at work. Hostile-environment harassment, quid pro quo harassment, a favor-for-a- favor harassment, and the person-to-person illegal dealing candy store business is an expensive legal battle in the court systems. The one word, prostitution, helps unlock the understanding for both, the managers and their employees. SEXUAL HARASSMENT IS also a book about getting help from counselors to redirect managers with issues with his or her leadership skills and social skills, seeking assistance from your EAP programs, and ambassador steps you have initiated internally. This book has addressed the need for easy-straightforward communication on sexual harassment. My goal is to help save companies thousands to possible millions in the future over sexual harassment lawsuits. The sooner the employee reports a hostile working environment the better off everyone will be. Every employee wants to be a valued employee, including this sexually harassed victim and now the author of this compelling book.

Sexual Harassment Is: A New Way of Thinking

As a company or firm operating in business, your financial wallets or checkbooks are open covering the expenses of the daily operations of business. Sexual harassment or prostitution on-the-

job can put a huge dent into the financial resources of a business. There are many high-tech electronic pieces of equipment that are available at very reasonable prices that can be used to investigate a claim about sexual harassment. For decades we have needed both, goodwill ambassadors to compassionately listen to a victim claiming a horrible sexual harassment encounter is occurring and the help from hidden cameras. Would a manager want his or her office environment monitored with a hidden camera for an investigation lasting six months to 18 months, after a claim of sexual harassment? No manager in their right mind would want that situation. The manager does not want to deal with an intense situation of being watched because of a sexual harassment or a prostitution claim. The employee does not want to deal with an intense situation of being sexually harassed. The tide has been turned at this point. No corrective action paperwork has been documented or placed into any manager's file, due to a claim against them over sexual harassment. The company is using an internal self-defense to guard millions in damages from lawsuits and guarding the safety of all the employees.

Sexual Harassment Is: Recommending More Options

In some special instances, hidden cameras are needed to add additional security in all areas of life; businesses, families, or homes. I have found using inexpensive cameras in my environment has given me back some control, some safety, and some more peace of mind. If you decide to incorporate 21st century high-tech hidden camera investigation technology into your workplace, formally communicate the usefulness of how the hidden camera monitoring equipment can or will be used to protect the careers of all employees. A false accusation made at work about SEXUAL HARASSMENT IS very damaging to the careers of managers and supervisors. The one word, prostitution, can easily provide some supervisors and managers the social will-power to want to avoid video or audio investigations. On the news I had heard one employee, who was being sexually harassed wore a hidden camera or microphone to work and delivered to the human resources department the evidence and complaint all at one time. The HR departments should lead the way and say yes your department will embrace new information and electronic

technology to help remove sexual harassment and create safer workplaces. Bullying and sexual harassment are two good reasons to add hidden cameras and mikes.

Some technology specialist employed at your companies can possibly work with the Human Resources department to implement some additional temporary non-detectable cameras, during an investigation or ask the employee complaining about the sexually harassment to wear a hidden camera. You may want to communicate in a formal company communication pamphlet; the company can or will only employ hidden cameras or mikes to investigate all accusations of sexual harassment or prostitution to protect both, the careers of the managers and the careers of the employees. Your company's financial wallets are open to share the financial success of your business to all your employees. Protecting your workplace environment from sexual harassment, prostitution, or bullying will benefit everyone. Sexual harassment information communicated simply may be beneficial in dealing with these unwanted sexual encounters and a few pieces of inexpensive hidden cameras can guard the valuables of your business. Integrity is valuable to a business. The safety of your employees working onsite is also another valuable item. I am offering some internal self-defense approaches to a very expensive and challenging problem in the workplace. These Internet web pages suggested below can change slightly, but the homepage or company name is listed in the Internet address below. I am providing information to assist you in your technology searches. So please do not get frustrated, if the exact page address changes, because companies will modify websites.

Hidden Camera Technology: Miscellaneous Places to Visit
http://www.homespy.com/
http://www.lightinthebox.com/
http://www.cctvcamerapros.com/

Thousands of employees are helpless to this attack. I needed to put into words the attacks of my experience. The person I had respected, as a boss, initiated a new dynamic to the working relationship. I felt the need to communicate I knew the

sexual harassment encounters were also a war waged against my ability to survive and earn a standard of living. I had to communicate all the elements involved, my job was now threatened, my professional career was being damaged, my paycheck is now a tool for sex, instead of the reward of working, and I had to fight back. Employees want to be heard and protected, also.

Teenagers working across America and around the world should be trained and equipped to handle these situations of the prostitution in the workplace. Our teenagers are not equipped to handle this battle. You and I can begin to change the lives of working teenagers. I believe an internal self-defense approach for everyone to address sexual harassment or prostitution in the workplace will benefit everyone. I have heard people speak about the human resources department protects the company only. I know I have felt that way and did not seek help all the time. I believe ambassadors in the Human Resources departments can be corporate America's greatest tool and first-line of internal self-defense in dealing with sexual harassment or prostitution on-the-job. I believe the term, goodwill ambassadors, communicates an open door to discuss these problems and get the help that is needed. I believe teaching this on-the-job prostitution, a shady invitation from a boss can be very insulting to some employees. I believe understanding this will change the workplace dynamics in a positive way. I believe equipping everyone with the tools necessary to deal with this problem of feeling prostituted at work will help both, the adults and teenagers in a positive way.

The one word, prostitution, in the workplace has a broader meaning. Some victims like me are translating or thinking the sexual harassment from the boss as; "All the cards are out on the table and you are asking me to: What?" The "invitation" from the boss was a true insult to many and a jaw dropper for some employees. The interpretation split from some employees might be 50%, 60% or 25%; a flattering pass, or a straight-out insult. There is a split in the interpretation and the other side wants to be heard. I believe the one word; prostitution, will give more managers or supervisors the social will-power to avoid starting this conflict in the workplace. I believe this book provides you, as an

employer or a parent another tool to discuss sexual harassment conflicts on-the-job. If you happen to be a parent, you have another self-defense tool to help protect your family's future. What greater tool could you give your employees to understand sexual harassment or prostitution on-the-job? What greater tool could you give a teenager working for you or living at home?

"Quid pro quo harassment" occurs when "submission to or rejection of such conduct by an individual is used as the basis for employment decisions affecting such individual. Hostile-environment harassment may acquire characteristics of "quid pro quo" harassment, if the offending supervisor abuses his authority over employment decisions to force the victim to endure or participate in the sexual conduct." (e).

PROMPT ACTION: If the Human Resources department guaranteed the sexual harassed victim an equal job position, or (e.g.), income for 18-24 months after reporting a verifiable sexual harassment claim in writing, this action communicates to the employee, his or her economic safety is number one, this reaffirms sexual acts are not required for company benefits, and

the employee can move forward feeling less threatened. If the Human Resources department intervened, as a goodwill ambassador, to reassure the employee's value, this would be a huge act of non-threatening arbitration. I believe the HR department can be goodwill ambassadors. This type of action could speak volumes in the court system. Motivate your employees to seek out his or her goodwill ambassadors in the Human Resources department immediately. A less hostile workplace is created and Human Resources Manager's actions can help to return some dignity of the sexually harassed employee. Equal opportunity and humane treatment are big agendas at many companies. If the employee signs a release with employment guarantees, that no whistleblower damages by the company will occur, both parties have saved money from damages and legal costs. If companies enacted aggressive non-threatening arbitration, how could the companies end up in the court system over sexual harassment over managers or supervisors? New frameworks for sexual harassment and prostitution, which are non-threatening arbitration, will help create a less hostile work environment. The protected employee would still have to meet the expectations of job performance like quality work and being on time, if the employee decides to remain with the company.

Many managers may find better will-power to avoid sexually harassing subordinates because of the nice goodwill packages provided to the victims from a goodwill ambassador in the Human Resources department. Some managers and supervisors will find greater will-power to avoid making an employee feel prostituted on-the-job from these two additional incentives, a hidden camera investigation in the workplace lasting six months to 18 months and the possibility of having prostitution on-the-job written down in his or her work record. Both, the company wins and the sexually harassed employee wins in the end. In this book, SEXUAL HARASSMENT IS, I am asking the managers and the supervisors to pause, step back, stop, and reflect on the subordinate employee's situation when placed into an encounter of sexual harassment, which then makes an employee feel like he or she is being asked to prostitute for a paycheck.

The numbers in destroyed lives from sexual harassment encounters can and should greatly turn around. Sexual harassment, the candy label has now been removed.

Goodwill ambassadors in Human Resources departments can help to change the lives of thousands of employees for decades to come. Goodwill ambassadors in the Human Resources department will be known for protecting both, the company's assets and the safety of all the employees equally. What if the sexual harassment legal cases in the courtrooms were cut in half? I think both, the companies and the employees together will be changing the statistics of feeling prostituted on-the-job. What a lovely picture, if the Human Resources departments around the world are now able to save more careers of the sexually harassed victims and save their companies more millions at the same time. Saving the careers of both, the adults and the teenagers will put a smile on everyone's face.

Sexual Harassment Is, Therapy in Your Hands Today

SEXUAL HARASSMENT IS therapy for the soul. The victims tell themselves how badly they were treated. The victims tell themselves how wrong those interactions they had to endure. The victims know that was a nightmare. My book is the therapy victims need. My books were a blessing to my soul and healing began when I started writing.

Chapter 2

The U.S. Equal Employment Opportunity Commission

Sexual Harassment – Definition (e)

"Title VII does not proscribe all conduct of a sexual nature in the workplace. Thus, it is crucial to clearly define sexual harassment: only unwelcome sexual conduct that is a term or condition of employment constitutes a violation" (e).

"29 C.F.R. _ 1604.11(a). The EEOC's Guidelines define two types of sexual harassment: "quid pro quo" and "hostile environment." The Guidelines provide that "unwelcome" sexual conduct constitutes sexual harassment when "submission to such conduct is made either explicitly or implicitly a term or condition of an individual's employment," (e).

"29 C.F.R _ 1604.11 (a) (1). "Quid pro quo harassment" occurs when "submission to or rejection of such conduct by an individual is used as the basis for employment decisions affecting such individual," (e).

"29 C.F.R _ 1604.11(a)(2).1 29 C.F.R. _ 1604.11(a)(3).2 The Supreme Court's decision in Vinson established that both types of sexual harassment are actionable under section 703 of Title VII of the Civil Rights Act of 1964", (e).

"42 U.S.C. _ 2000e-2(a), as forms of sex discrimination" (e).

"Although "quid pro quo" and "hostile environment" harassment are theoretically distinct claims, the line between the two is not always clear and the two forms of harassment often occur together. For example, an employee's tangible job conditions are affected when a sexually hostile work environment results in her constructive discharge.3 Similarly, a supervisor who makes sexual advances toward a subordinate employee may communicate an implicit threat to adversely affect her job status if she does not comply. "Hostile environment" harassment may acquire characteristics of "quid pro quo" harassment if the offending supervisor abuses his authority over employment decisions to force the victim to endure or participate in the sexual conduct. Sexual harassment may culminate in a retaliatory discharge if a victim tells the harasser or her employer she will no longer submit to the harassment, and is then fired in retaliation for this protest. Under these circumstances it would be appropriate to conclude that both harassment and retaliation in violation of section 704(a) of Title VII have occurred" (e).

"Distinguishing between the two types of harassment is necessary when determining the employer's liability (see infra Section D). But while categorizing sexual harassment as "quid pro quo," "hostile environment," or both is useful analytically these distinctions should not limit the Commission's investigations,4 which generally should consider all available evidence and testimony under all possibly applicable theories[5]" (e).

- "determining whether sexual conduct is "unwelcome";

- evaluating evidence of harassment;

- determining whether a work environment is sexually "hostile";

- holding employers liable for sexual harassment by supervisors; and

- evaluating preventive and remedial action taken in response to claims of sexual harassment" (e).

REFERENCES

(a) Merriam-Webster, Incorporated, Solicit,(2009), http://www.merriam-webster.com/dictionary/solicit

(b) Merriam-Webster, Incorporated, Prostitute,(2009), http://www.merriam-webster.com/dictionary/prostitute

(c) Merriam-Webster, Incorporated, Debase,(2009), http://www.merriam-webster.com/dictionary/debase

(d) Merriam-Webster, Incorporated, Sexual harassment,(2009), http://m-w.com/dictionary/sexual%20harassment

(e) The U.S. Equal Employment Opportunity Commission, Retrieved December 2009,
    http://www.eeoc.gov/policy/docs/currentissues.html

www.ingramcontent.com/pod-product-compliance
Lightning Source LLC
Chambersburg PA
CBHW071308280526
45788CB00004B/1855